startled and confused its contemporary readership and still causes us to reflect on our conventional notions of what constitutes the genre of the love story. In the central relationship between Catherine and Heathcliff, Brontë takes the sweep of idealised romance for example and fuses it with **gothic** fantasy and horror. In the comfortable domestic realism of Catherine's marriage to Edgar, Brontë interleaves a discourse of illness and childbirth which eventually leads to death.

Narcissism characterises the relationship between Isabella and Heathcliff, and similarly that between Catherine and Edgar. When Heathcliff's love of Catherine corrupts into a lust for revenge, his passion transgresses powerful social taboos: he lies with her dead body in the grave; he tyrannises his dying son in order to accumulate wealth; and he abuses his wife gratuitously and without compunction. Catherine, unable to reconcile her passion for Heathcliff with her marriage to Edgar resorts to self-destruction: 'I'll try to break their hearts by breaking my own' (p. 116). She refuses food, willfully exposes herself to a chill when she is feverish and works herself up into a nervous agitation while she is carrying Edgar's child. She dies in childbirth, and her daughter is born two months premature. The greatest of love stories, then, is explored through the profoundest acts of violence.

NATURE AND CULTURE

The dichotomy between nature and culture, which forms part of the thematic structure of this novel, is played out in the relationship between the two houses: Wuthering Heights, which represents nature and Thrushcross Grange representing culture. The theme is developed in the ways in which the houses similarly represent enclosure or exposure. The opposition between these two displays them as both antagonistic and subtly matched. This is a conflict that can be interpreted in a number of ways: in historical terms as a rural way of life contends against industrialisation; in psychological terms as a struggle between the ego and the id; in sexual terms as a choice between experience and representation.

The representations of nature in this novel are almost invariably brutal or hostile. From the very beginning Lockwood identifies himself as a man of culture, appropriately living at the Grange, and utterly incapable of reading the signs of nature. His abortive attempt to negotiate the snowstorm and read the human signs which underlie the elements are testimony to this.

Nature is neither legible, nor representable in this novel. Lockwood cannot read its signs, and Catherine refuses to name it. Nor is nature seen as unremittingly cruel in comparison to culture. The representations of culture see it as equally dangerous, and violent.

Morality

There are at least three views of morality which are pitted against each other in this novel. Conventional, institutionalised morality might be said to be most forcibly represented by Joseph, and it is represented as pious, restrictive, domineering and legislative. Ever ready with a Biblical quotation or religious homily, Joseph provides a relentlessly sour commentary upon the activities of the other members of the Heights household. His is the restrictive voice of social convention which intrudes upon this house of nature, regulating it and judging it.

The second form of morality which is explored in the novel focuses attention upon the morality of authenticity, of being true to the self. In the light of this morality, Catherine's marriage to Edgar is judged as an extreme act of bad faith which precipitates all subsequent tragedy and evil.

The third form of morality which is explored is that of self-interest over altruism. Many of the characters in the novel appear to act for the good of others, and yet their actions serve the aggrandisement of their own power or knowledge. For example, Nelly Dean withholds or reveals her knowledge apparently arbitrarily, but her choices to do so invariably influence the events of the novel. Examples of this are when she neglects to tell Edgar about Catherine's illness and when she informs him of Cathy's correspondence with Linton. On each occasion her decision has profound consequences for the events of the novel.

Education

Brontë seems ambivalent about the effects of education. The denial of education to Heathcliff is perceived as a form of social punishment and humiliation. It robs Heathcliff of status both within the family and within society. Yet Hareton's painful acquisition of a formal education in the final part of the novel can be read as having both beneficial and negative implications. Hareton acquires the learning and social skills required for union with Cathy; but he also appears to lose power – including sexual power – in his submission to this option. This might be read in terms of a repetition of Catherine's choice earlier in the text, where she trades authentic selfhood for social privilege.

Education in the form of reading, however, dignifies Nelly Dean in her role as narrator and lends her social status.

IMAGERY AND SYMBOLISM

BOUNDARIES

A number of critics have commented on the novel's emphasis upon physical boundaries like walls, windows, locks, gates and doorways. Throughout the novel these boundaries are both defended and breached. Lockwood is barred from the Heights when he first visits; he then attempts to bar Cathy's ghost; Catherine and Heathcliff are barred from Thrushcross Grange; Each character seeks control by locking others in or out, each episode details some imprisonment or exclusion. Overall, however, the novel documents the futility of every such attempt.

Dorothy Van Ghent has famously argued that the various windows and barriers serve both to separate and connect polar opposites: inside and outside; human and ghost. However, all the enclosures are violated. No boundary remains intact, neither property, nor bedroom, nor body, nor book, nor grave, nor dream. The contradictions exist in a tension which is both compelling and fragile, threatening and vulnerable.

TEXTUALITY

This is a novel which abounds with texts, from Catherine's diaries, to Joseph's biblical quotations, from the books in the Thrushcross Grange library which keep Edgar occupied while Catherine is dying to the books which Hareton hurls into the fire in his public humiliation. Letters too form a crucial part of the action of the novel, pushing events forward and aiding character development.

Our first introduction to Wuthering Heights as a building is via the inscription that sits above the door. Within the novel each text might be seen to represent the heterogeneity of the whole, for none of the various texts correspond with each other: even the letters which pass between the various characters fail to communicate. Each text stands as a testimony to contradiction, to supplementarity, to the impossibility of uncontestable readings.

As J. Hillis Miller has observed, the novel comes to the reader packaged in text, in terms of its innumerable prefaces and introductions. Such presentation is now so standard that it is difficult to negotiate the end of one text and the beginning of the next, or the novel proper.

Wuthering Heights is a novel which is rich in **semiotics**. It abounds with a superabundance of signs, from the gravestones (standing as a sign of absence) to the memoranda of Catherine that Heathcliff sees in everything around him.

Animal imagery

Brontë frequently uses animal imagery as a metaphor for some human frailty or moral deficiency: Linton, for example is described as a 'chicken' (p. 205), Hareton a 'dog' (p. 307), Heathcliff a 'mad dog' (p. 160), 'savage beast' (p. 167). Lockwood's mistaken apprehension of a heap of dead rabbits for a chairful of cats not only identifies him as unobservant, but also someone who is incapable of reading animal imagery and, given the preponderance of such imagery in this novel, it is therefore entirely appropriate that his narratorial role is quickly taken over by Nelly Dean.

Dreams

Dreams are an important key to knowledge in this novel, and the dreamwork and hallucinatory elements of the text have anticipated twentieth-century **psychoanalytic criticism**.

Dreams demonstrate a way of thinking through the forbidden. They are equipped with a magic all their own. In the novel, dreams are clearly of central importance and their relation to magic, to visions, to ghostly apparitions is never understated.

Lockwood's dream of the child Cathy begging to be let in is disturbing on two levels. It is grisly, and the gratuitous cruelty of him sawing her wrist against the broken glass is uncomfortable. But as Frank Kermode suggests, it is also disturbing because neither Lockwood nor Heathcliff really believe that it was a dream. It therefore doubly resists integration into the rational.

LANGUAGE AND STYLE

DIALECT

Brontë's use of the Yorkshire dialect has generally been considered to be an accurate rendition of the accent. In the second edition of the novel, which was edited and amended by Charlotte Brontë, Charlotte modified the rendering of Joseph's dialect in order to make it more comprehensible. Over time, Charlotte's edition has fallen from favour and most modern editions now take the first edition as their starting point. However, this use of dialect possibly earned Brontë's novel some of its early censure, since the language and manners of the local characters were criticised for being rough and coarse.

POETIC LANGUAGE

The superabundance of metaphor and symbol and the lyricism of the descriptive passages have earned this novel praise for its poetic language:

> One time, however, we were near quarrelling. He said the pleasantest manner of spending a hot July day was lying from morning till evening on a bank of heath in the middle of the moors, with the bees humming dreamily about among the bloom, and the larks singing high up over head, and the blue sky, and bright sun shining steadily and cloudlessly. That was his most perfect idea of heaven's happiness – mine was rocking in a rustling green tree, with a west wind blowing, and bright, white clouds flitting rapidly above; and not only larks, but throstles, and blackbirds, and linnets, and cuckoos pouring out music on every side, and the moors seen at a distance, broken into cool, dusky dells; but close by great swells of long grass

undulating in waves to the breeze; and the woods and sounding water, and the whole world awake and wild with joy. He wanted all to lie in an ecstasy of peace; I wanted all to sparkle, and dance in a glorious jubilee. (p. 245)

DUAL NARRATION

Brontë frames her narrative in terms of a dual narration, a technique that was virtually unprecedented when she wrote *Wuthering Heights*. Her first narrator Lockwood is demonstrably unreliable: he mistakes social relationships and radically misreads Heathcliff from the beginning. Although Nelly Dean's narrative is somewhat less subject to contradiction and denial, it is nevertheless evidently informed by her own partiality, and from time to time her ulterior motives. We are never under the illusion Nelly Dean's is a neutral or objective narrative. The novel explicitly resists such consolations and insists upon the responsibilities of all readers and storytellers.

PART FOUR

TEXTUAL ANALYSIS

TEXT 1 (PAGES 25–6)

I listened doubtingly an instant; detected the disturber, then turned and dozed and dreamt again; if possible, still more disagreeably than before.

This time I remembered I was lying in the oak closet, and I heard distinctly the gusty wind and the driving of the snow; I heard, also the fir-bough repeat its teasing sound, and ascribed it to the right cause: but, it annoyed me so much, that I resolved to silence it, if possible; and, I thought, I rose and endeavoured to unhasp the casement. The hook was soldered into the staple, a circumstance observed by me, when awake, but forgotten.

'I must stop it, nevertheless!' I muttered, knocking my knuckles through the glass, and stretching an arm out to seize the importunate branch: instead of which, my fingers closed on the fingers of a little, ice-cold hand!

The intense horror of nightmare came over me; I tried to draw back my arm, but, the hand clung to it, and a most melancholy voice sobbed,

'Let me in – let me in!'

'Who are you?' I asked, struggling, meanwhile, to disengage myself.

'Catherine Linton,' it replied, shiveringly (why did I think of *Linton*? I had read *Earnshaw* twenty times for Linton). 'I'm come home, I'd lost my way on the moor!'

As it spoke, I discerned, obscurely, a child's face looking through the window – Terror made me cruel; and, finding it useless to attempt to shake the creature off, I pulled its wrist on to the broken pane and rubbed it to and fro till the blood ran down and soaked the bed-clothes: still it wailed, 'Let me in!' and maintained its tenacious gripe, almost maddening me with fear.

'How can I?' I said at length. 'Let *me* go, if you want me to let you in!'

The fingers relaxed, I snatched mine through the hole, hurriedly piled the books up in a pyramid against it, and stopped my ears to exclude the lamentable prayer.

I seemed to keep them closed above a quarter of an hour, yet, the instant I listened again, there was a doleful cry moaning on!

'Begone!' I shouted, 'I'll never let you in, not if you beg for twenty years!'

'It's twenty years,' mourned the voice, 'twenty years, I've been a waif for twenty years!'

Thereat began a feeble scratching outside, and the pile of books moved as if thrust forward.

I tried to jump up; but, could not stir a limb; and so yelled aloud, in a frenzy of fright.

To my confusion, I discovered the yell was not ideal. Hasty footsteps approached my chamber door: somebody pushed it open, with a vigorous hand, and a light glimmered through the squares at the top of the bed. I sat shuddering yet, and wiping the perspiration from my forehead: the intruder appeared to hesitate and muttered to himself.

At last, he said in a half-whisper, plainly not expecting an answer,

'Is any one here?'

I considered it best to confess my presence, for I knew Heathcliff's accents, and feared he might search further, if I kept quiet.

With this intention, I turned and opened the panels – I shall not soon forget the effect my action produced.

Heathcliff stood near the entrance, in his shirt and trousers; with a candle dripping over his fingers, and his face as white as the wall behind him. The first creak of the oak startled him like an electric shock: the light leaped from his hold to a distance of some feet, and his agitation was so extreme, that he could hardly pick it up.

'It is only your guest, sir,' I called out, desirous to spare him the humiliation of exposing his cowardice further. 'I had the misfortune to scream in my sleep, owing to a frightful nightmare. I'm sorry I disturbed you.'

'Oh, God confound you, Mr Lockwood! I wish you were at the –'

commenced my host, setting the candle on a chair because he found it impossible to hold it steady.

The passage, coming from the beginning of the novel, before Lockwood relinquishes his narration, exemplifies some of the important issues of the novel. This dream and its predecessor have been the focus of much critical attention. This is the first time that we encounter Catherine, and though she appears as a ghostly child, she identifies herself as Linton, which the usually impercipient Lockwood parenthetically notes. This establishes one of the central themes of the novel, the uncertain nature of identity and belonging. The equivocacy that is associated here with the name reflects the confusion of the repetitious doubling of names in this novel. If naming is central to identity then the paucity of names in the text suggests that identity is multiple and historical rather than individual and unique.

It is a passage which is self-consciously horrific. It is significant that Lockwood suggests that terror made him cruel, since he has just previously been reading Catherine's diary in which she describes the day that she and Heathcliff first peep in on Thrushcross Grange, where Lockwood now properly resides. The outcome of this encounter is that Catherine is savaged by the Lintons' dogs, after she and Heathcliff had 'terrif[ied]' the Linton children by making 'frightful noises' (p. 49). This association of violence with civilisation is not insignificant and requires to be read against the assumption that the violence of this novel associates solely and powerfully with Heathcliff and Wuthering Heights. It is worth bearing in mind that our initial encounters with terror in the novel are intimately associated with Thrushcross Grange, and the relationship between the Grange and the Heights.

It is also worth noting from this passage the inadequacy of the books to protect Lockwood from the encroaching terror, which he rationalises at the beginning of the dream as nature. This again is indicative of a central theme in the novel: the conflict between nature and culture.

The fact that Lockwood breaks the glass between the spirit world and his own can be read metaphorically as a transgressive act. Here he breaks through the barriers of propriety that separate one worldview from another. It is one example of the kinds of violation that have lead to this novel being deemed so subversive.

Finally, it is worth commenting how Lockwood erroneously transfers his own feelings of fear and humiliation onto Heathcliff. This repeats his initial inclination to assume that they are similar in temperament, and also indicates Lockwood's unwavering belief that his own conventional worldview and experience of the world are common to everyone; that his is a neutral, unbiased and utterly rational interpretation of events. This vastly egocentric position is something, perhaps, that the radically unconnected nature of Heathcliff encourages in others. The facility which permits Heathcliff to reinvent himself also permits others to project their inventions onto him. For example, it characterises Isabella's relationship with him, where she disastrously extrapolates her own version of the **Byronic hero,** and similarly Catherine repeats the error, when she fails to comprehend that her decision to marry Edgar might have any detrimental effect upon her relationship with Heathcliff.

TEXT 2   (PAGES 80–1)

'I was only going to say that heaven did not seem to be my home; and I broke my heart with weeping to come back to earth; and the angels were so angry that they flung me out, into the middle of the heath on the top of Wuthering Heights; where I woke sobbing for joy … I've no more business to marry Edgar Linton than I have to be in heaven; and if the wicked man in there had not brought Heathcliff so low, I shouldn't have thought of it. It would degrade me to marry Heathcliff, now; so he shall never know how I love him; and that, not because he's handsome, Nelly, but because he's more myself than I am. Whatever our souls are made of, his and mine are the same, and Linton's is as different as a moonbeam from lightning, or frost from fire.'

Ere this speech ended I became sensible of Heathcliff's presence. Having noticed a slight movement, I turned my head, and saw him rise from the bench and steal out, noiselessly. He had listened till he heard Catherine say it would degrade her to marry him, and then he staid to hear no farther …

'… Heathcliff has no notion of these things … He does not know what being in love is?'

'I see no reason that he should not know, as well as you,' I returned; 'and if *you* are his choice, he'll be the most unfortunate creature that ever was born! As soon as you become Mrs Linton, he loses friend, and love, and all! Have you considered how you'll bear the separation, and how he'll bear to be quite deserted in the world? Because, Miss Catherine –'

'He quite deserted! we separated!' she exclaimed, with an accent of indignation. 'Who is to separate us, pray? They'll meet the fate of Milo! Not as long as I live, Ellen – for no mortal creature. Every Linton on the face of the earth might melt into nothing, before I could consent to forsake Heathcliff. Oh, that's not what I intend – that's not what I mean! I shouldn't be Mrs Linton were such a price demanded! He'll be as much to me as he has been all his lifetime. Edgar must shake off his antipathy, and tolerate him, at least. He will when he learns my true feelings towards him. Nelly, I see now, you think me a selfish wretch, but, did it never strike you that, if Heathcliff and I married, we should be beggars? whereas, if I marry Linton, I can aid Heathcliff to rise, and place him out of my brother's power … This is for the sake of one who comprehends in his person my feelings to Edgar and myself. I cannot express it; but surely you and every body have a notion that there is, or should be, an existence of yours beyond you. What were the use of creation if I were entirely contained here? My great miseries in this world have been Heathcliff's miseries, and I watched and felt each from the beginning; my great thought in living is himself. If all else perished, and *he* remained, I should still continue to be; and if all else remained, and he were annihilated, the Universe would turn to a mighty stranger. I should not seem a part of it. My love for Linton is like the foliage in the woods. Time will change it, I'm well aware, as winter changes the trees – my love for Heathcliff resembles the eternal rocks beneath – a source of little visible delight, but necessary. Nelly, I *am* Heathcliff – he's always, always in my mind – not as a pleasure, any more than I am always a pleasure to myself – but as my own being – so don't talk of our separation again – it is impracticable; and –'

Possibly the most famous passage in the novel, Catherine here declares her love for Heathcliff in the most extravagant and arresting of terms.

The passage highlights some of the central thematic oppositions in the novel: joy and redemption; belonging and exclusion; constancy and transience; expediency and struggle. These oppositions contend against each other in an unresolvable tension throughout the novel.

Once again the passage can be seen to deal with issues of identity and individuality, and it does so in cosmological and religious terms. Brontë wrestles with the profoundly existential question of what happens to the notion of the individual when one is in love? It is a question of wide-ranging theological and social implications. The union between herself and Heathcliff Catherine perceives to preclude her from heaven, and although she suggests that it similarly precludes her from marriage to Edgar Linton, she ignores this and goes on to detail an elaborate rationalisation of her proposed marriage. Such a rationalisation, while it is in direct conflict with her passion for Heathcliff, and threatens to annihilate him, is nevertheless entirely within the bounds of propriety associated with the social contract of marriage. As a daughter who could not expect to inherit any property, Catherine rightly comments that her economic and social survival depends on marriage. The central choice of the novel, then can be read as a stark choice about survival. Catherine recognises that without Heathcliff she could not exist as herself, but that without a legitimate social role and position neither she nor Heathcliff could live.

Catherine's assertion that were Heathcliff to be annihilated the Universe would turn to a mighty stranger seems to echo her poem 'No Coward Soul'.

Although this is the most dramatic instance of these issues, it is not the only intimation that the ideal relationship cannot be sustained. It echoes Lockwood's confession of being unworthy of a comfortable home on p. 6, and it is also given its inversion in Isabella's fantastic declaration of the potential of her relationship with Heathcliff on pp. 100–3.

TEXT 3   (PAGES 304–5)

Before I arrived in sight of it, all that remained of day was a beamless, amber light along the west; but I could see every pebble on the path and every blade of grass, by that splendid moon.

I had neither to climb the gate, nor to knock – it yielded to my hand.

That is an improvement! I thought. And I noticed another, by the aid of my nostrils; a fragrance of stocks and wall flowers, wafted on the air, from amongst the homely fruit trees.

Both doors and lattices were open; and yet, as is usually the case in a coal district, a fine, red fire illumined the chimney; the comfort which the eye derives from it, renders the extra heat endurable. But the house of Wuthering Heights is so large, that the inmates have plenty of space for withdrawing out of its influence; and. accordingly, what inmates there were had stationed themselves not far from one of the windows. I could both see them and hear them talk before I entered; and looked and listened in consequence, being moved thereto by a mingled sense of curiosity, and envy that grew as I lingered.

'Con-*trary!*' said a voice as sweet as a silver bell – 'That for the third time, you dunce! I'm not going to tell you again – Recollect, or I pull your hair!'

'Contrary, then,' answered another, in deep, but softened tones. 'And now, kiss me for minding so well.'

'No, read it over first correctly, without a single mistake.'

The male speaker began to read – he was a young man, respectably dressed, and seated at a table, having a book before him. His handsome features glowed with pleasure, and his eyes kept impatiently wandering from the page to a small white hand over his shoulder, which recalled him by a smart slap on the cheek, whenever its owner detected such signs of inattention.

Its owner stood behind; her light shining ringlets blending, at intervals, with his brown locks, as she bent to superintend his studies; and her face – it was lucky he could not see her face, or he would never have been so steady – I could, and I bit my lip, in spite, at having thrown away the chance I might have had, of doing something besides staring at its smiting beauty.

The task was done, not free from further blunders, but the pupil claimed a reward and received at least five kisses, which, however, he generously returned. Then, they came to the door, and from their conversation, I judged they were about to issue out and have a walk on the moors. I supposed I should be condemned in Hareton Earnshaw's heart, if not by his mouth, to the lowest pit in the infernal regions if I showed my unfortunate person in his neighbourhood then, and feeling very mean and malignant, I skulked round to seek refuge in the kitchen.

There was unobstructed admittance on that side also; and, at the door, sat my old friend, Nelly Dean, sewing and singing a song, which was often interrupted from within, by harsh words of scorn and intolerance, uttered in far from musical accents. 'Aw'd rayther, by th'haulf, hev 'em swearing i'my lugs frough morn tuh neeght, nur hearken yah, hahsiver!' said the tenant of the kitchen, in answer to an unheard speech of Nelly's. 'It's a blazing shaime, ut Aw cannut oppen t' Blessed Book, bud yah set up them glories tuh sattan, un' all t'flaysome wickednesses ut iver wer born intuh t'warld! Oh! yah're a raight nowt; un shoo's another; un that poor lad 'ull be lost, atween ye ...'

'... wisht, old man, and read your Bible, like a Christian, and never mind me. This is "Fairy Annie's Wedding" – a bonny tune – it goes to a dance.'

This passage, taken from the last section of the novel, when the narrative has once more returned to Lockwood, revisits some of the major issues of the novel. The opening paragraph to the passage revises Lockwood's primary encounter with the moors, which he prophetically calls 'a perfect misanthropist's Heaven!' (p. 3). By now we are to assume that he can read the signs of nature in a way that he was almost fatally unable to do earlier in the text.

Significantly the barriers of the house are open to him now, and he gains easy access to the house. Equally significantly he chooses not to enter straight away, but to linger outside and observe. This echoes his earlier account of voyeuristic pleasure when he describes admiring 'a real goddess' (p. 6). Following the conventions established in the novel for reading the two houses we can now observe with Lockwood that Wuthering Heights has accommodated a reconciliation between culture and nature. This is further emphasised by the scent of cultivated flowers, which can be read as both leisure and sensual pleasure, growing alongside the fruit trees, which can be read as both knowledge and nourishment.

The passage also provides commentary on the theme of education. Hareton here apparently enjoys acquiring the skills which will equip him for marriage into property, but not without paying the price of subjugating his masculinity to the restraining white hand of female coercion.

The association of love and heaven is once again rescripted, both in Lockwood's assumption that Hareton would condemn him to hell, and in the sanctimonious and similarly ungenerous grumbling of Joseph. Against these **discourses** of religion, education and restrained desire is pitted Nelly Dean's song, significantly titled 'Fairy Annie's Wedding' which reintroduces folklore and fantasy as equally legitimate forms of knowledge. This choice of song might also be read as signalling the impossibly fairytale nature of the impending marriage between the two houses.

The passage offers an example of Brontë's use of dialect, which has been noted for its authenticity. Here it serves to signify clan and cultural knowledge, signalling both Lockwood's inability to shake off prejudice and Joseph's tenacious grip on a way of life that was already besieged by other nineteenth-century discourses of science and industrialisation.

PART FIVE

BACKGROUND

EMILY BRONTË

Emily Brontë was born in 1818 in Yorkshire. Her father, Patrick Brontë, was curate of Haworth Parsonage. In 1821 Emily's mother died and, following the deaths of two elder sisters in 1825 the surviving children, Charlotte, Emily, Anne and Branwell were brought up by their aunt in the parsonage. They lived relatively remotely from their community, and Charlotte explains in the biographical notice which prefaces most editions of the text, that they took their chief enjoyment from literary compositions which they invented for each other most famously the sagas of the mythical island of Gondal which inspired their later poetry. Patrick Brontë fostered in his children a spirit of intellectual enquiry and a love of literature, they had access to his library and to the nearby library in Keighley. Emily briefly attended Cowan Bridge School and went to Row Head in 1835

Following Charlotte's discovery of her poetry notebooks Emily agreed to publish a book of poems jointly with her sisters, which they published in 1846 under the **pseudonyms** Currer, Ellis and Acton Bell.

Wuthering Heights is Emily's only novel and was published under the pseudonym Ellis Bell in 1847, a year before her death from tuberculosis.

HER OTHER WORKS

Emily Brontë published only one other work during her lifetime, which was a joint publication of poetry with her sisters. Although this book did not achieve critical acclaim, Charlotte remained convinced of the quality of Emily's verse and in the 1850 edition of *Wuthering Heights*, included some of Emily's verse as an appendix. This brought it to the attention of many readers, including the American poet Emily Dickinson (1830–86), who particularly admired the poem 'No Coward Soul', which was read at Dickinson's funeral. This inclusion of the poetry with the novel focused readers' attention on the poetic qualities of her prose writing.

Although critics are divided in their opinions as to the usefulness of an historical context for an understanding of *Wuthering Heights*, some, like Terry Eagleton, Arnold Kettle and Nancy Armstrong have focused acute critical attention upon the economic and social conditions which inform the novel, seeing the novel as both a product of and participant in the social context.

Certainly, Victorian readers would have been familiar with the story of Heathcliff as a foundling from the port of Liverpool: orphans and child beggars were a common enough social problem. Heathcliff's background, tantalisingly obscure as it might seem within the novel, can be read against the social upheavals of the mid nineteenth century, which saw unemployment as a result of industrialisation; the Irish potato famine which brought thousands of refugees to Liverpool; the decay of a rural lifestyle in the face of increased urbanisation and new technology. The **romantic** and nostalgic references to nature and to the moors as a place of childhood might also be read in this context. However, as Eva Figes points out in *Sex and Subterfuge, Women Writers in 1850* (Pandora, 1982) Victorian women writers had been largely prevented from writing social or political criticism in their novels owing to their vulnerable position as women writers. The rural setting of *Wuthering Heights* can be seen as indicative of the position of women as isolated from culture and modern industry. The emphasis upon the struggle between nature and culture, north and south, folklore and science, can be recognised as being particularly disturbing to its contemporary readership.

Emphasis upon a literary context for the novel has been twofold. First, critics have pointed out the poetic qualities of the novel and have cited the influence of Byron. Indeed it has become a critical commonplace to read Heathcliff as a **Byronic hero**. The Byronic influences have been particularly discussed by Winifred Gérin in her biography of Brontë. A second source of influence has been considered to be the **gothic** romance, and critics have seen the influence of ghosts and visions in this context. The gothic romance was a popular form of writing in the late 18th and 19th centuries. It generally dealt with the supernatural and the fantastic. Heathcliff's desire for Catherine which extends beyond the grave can be seen in this context. Gilbert and Gubar famously suggest the possibility of *Wuthering Heights* as a 'deliberate copy' of Mary Shelley's *Frankenstein*. Nancy Armstrong, though, suggests that such phenomena might also be read in terms of the competing discourses of folklore and literature.

PART SIX

CRITICAL HISTORY

RECEPTION AND EARLY REVIEWS

Early reviews of the novel praised it for its imaginative potency while criticising it for being strange and ambiguous. In a biographical notice attached to many modern versions of the novel, Charlotte Brontë complains that the novel did not receive sufficient merit in its initial reception. But *Wuthering Heights* did not go unrecognised by its early readers. Literary critics repeatedly acknowledged its originality, genius and imaginative power – if they also complained about its moral ambiguity.

CRITICAL HISTORY

Wuthering Heights is a novel which has generated enormous critical attention. It is impossible here to give an account of everything that has been written and said about this novel. Doubtless, there are some important omissions but the review attempts to give a representative overview of some of the positions that it is possible to take up in relation to the text Charlotte Brontë's **romantic** explanation of Emily Brontë as an inspired genius has led many critics to search for the unconscious or hidden meaning of *Wuthering Heights*; it has influenced **psychoanalytic criticism** and certain kinds of **formalist** and **feminist** criticism.

Following Charlotte's lead, some nineteenth-century analyses of *Wuthering Heights* emphasised the psychological elements of the novel's plot and characters. The critic Sydney Dobell praised Emily Brontë for her portrayal of the 'deep unconscious' truth of Catherine Earnshaw's personality (E. Jolly, ed., *The Life and Letters of Sydney Dobell*, pp. 169–74). According to Dobell, Brontë understood that 'certain crimes and sorrows are not so much the result of intrinsic evil as of a false position in the scheme of things'. A view that anticipates some **feminist** discussions of Catherine's choice.

Much early criticism tended to look to Brontë's life to understand elements in her work. For example, critics attempted to draw parallels between Brontë's depiction of Heathcliff and her brother Branwell. Such criticism is based on a view that the relationship between literature and the world is relatively straightforward, that reality exists and that it is literature's job to describe it. The role of literary criticism, according to this view, is to assess the accuracy of the representations, and also to assess the moral content of the work, for literature and the arts in general were held to be an integral part of the civilised life, and thus should contribute to the moral fabric of society.

Not all early criticism, however, focused exclusively on the moral or biographical aspects of the text. Some early critics focused on the novel's relationship to other literary texts. A review in *The Examiner* in 1848 noted that Heathcliff was a **Byronic hero**. More sophisticated contemporary versions of this approach include Gilbert and Gubar's reading in *The Madwoman in the Attic* where they read the novel as a revision of the Miltonic myth of the Fall and Harold Bloom's reading of the novel as a critique of Byron's *Manfred*. Such readings see literature as part of the real life we lead, not just reflective of it, and argue that the literary texts we create respond to and modify those we have read.

Close attention to Brontë's novel begins with C.P. Sanger's *The Structure of Wuthering Heights* (Hogarth, 1926) and Lord David Cecil's *Early Victorian Novelists* (Constable, 1935) both of whom wished to distance criticism from moral judgement and proceed from an analysis of the formal elements of the text. In this they prepared the way for the **new critics** such as Mark Schorer. Schorer sees the novel as a moral story about the futility of grand passion. Other new critics include Dorothy Van Ghent, who drew attention to the metaphors of windows and thresholds (see Theme on Boundaries).

Contemporary criticism has tended to move on from such approaches. **Feminist** criticism has seen the novel in terms of its language, and in terms of the strategies and opportunities that are open to women in the novel. **Feminist** and gender criticism has also provided some interesting readings of the ambivalent representations of gender in *Wuthering Heights*, not the least of which is Gilbert and Gubar's reading of Heathcliff as 'female' in the sense that second sons, bastards and daughters are female. Heathcliff is 'female' because he is dispossessed of social power. He has no status, no social place and no property. He is only Heathcliff, never Mr Heathcliff, or the Master, in contrast to Edgar Linton.

Heathcliff's rebellions against the social conventions of class, marriage and inheritance similarly suggest that he can be read as 'female' since endorsing such conventions only serves the interests of patriachial culture.

Marxist criticism has seen the novel in terms of its social relations, looking for the correspondences between the novel and the political, social and economic conditions under which it was produced. Arnold Kettle in *An Introduction to the English Novel* argues that the values represented in *Wuthering Heights*, against which Heathcliff rebels, reflect the specific tyranny of Victorian capitalist society. Perhaps the most famous Marxist analysis of the novel is given by Terry Eagleton in *Myths of Power: A Marxist Study of the Brontës* in which he considers the novel in terms of its reference to class, economics and history. Furthermore, Eagleton is interested in the novel's relationship to its culture's **ideology**, looking at how that ideology is both reflected and produced by the novel.

J. Hillis Miller has provided an influential deconstructive reading of the novel. **Deconstruction** offers an alternative to traditional scholarship which is both playful and openly adversarial. Unwilling to privilege a certain kind of reading, deconstructive criticism argues that there is no one right way to read a text, that literature does not contain the kinds of unified and universal truths that traditional criticism seeks. Instead deconstructive criticism considers the way in which all **transcendental** truths, including those judgements we might make about the aesthetic unity of the text, the inherent truth of the narrative, undo themselves in internal contradictions and incompatibilities. Miller's reading focuses upon the ways in which the novel resists rational explanation.

CONTEMPORARY APPROACHES

MARXIST

Marxist criticisms of *Wuthering Heights* include Terry Eagleton's *Myths of Power: A Marxist Study of the Brontës*; Arnold Kettle's *An Introduction to the English Novel*; Margaret Lenta's essay 'Capitalism or Patriarchy and Immoral Love: A Study of *Wuthering Heights*'; Raymond Williams's *The English Novel from Dickens to Lawrence* and David Wilson's essay 'Emily Brontë: First of the Moderns'.

Terry Eagleton considers the novel in terms of its relationship to **ideology**. He uses Lucien Goldmann's definition of the term, which he admits is suspect, but, in terms of assessing *Wuthering Heights*, useful. Goldmann's definition is that ideology signifies a false, incomplete, distortive or partial consciousness, which he opposes to the term 'world-view' which designates a true, total and coherent understanding of social relations.

Wuthering Heights, argues Eagleton presents a 'world-view', in that it is unfragmented by the conflicts that it represents. Contradictions and contesting oppositions coexist in this novel in a profound but not unsatisfying tension.

The primary contradiction that Eagleton explores in relation to this assertion is the choice that Catherine must make between Edgar Linton and Heathcliff. He identifies that choice as the pivotal event of the novel and the precipitating factor in all the tragic events which follow. Catherine chooses Edgar Linton, which Eagleton identifies as an act of 'bad faith', because of his social superiority, and she is, he judges, rightly criticised by Heathcliff for this betrayal of their more authentic love. The social self, Eagleton argues, is demonstrated as false not because it is only apparent, Catherine's love for Edgar is not simulated, but because it exists in a contradictory and negative relationship to authentic selfhood, which is her love of Heathcliff.

Eagleton's essay also analyses Heathcliff's position in the novel in terms of his place in the family structure, local society and the economic system of rural Yorkshire at the turn of the century. Because Heathcliff is spirited out of nowhere into this family, he has no social or domestic status, and he is therefore both a threat to the established order and an opportunity for it to be reinvented. Heathcliff disturbs the establishment because he has no legitimate place in its system. Eagleton's analysis turns on the issue of liberty and oppression. The fact that there is no opportunity for freedom either within or outside the system is a consequence of bourgeois society.

Heathcliff learns to see culture as a mode of oppression, and he acquires it to use as a weapon. This association of culture with violence is further played out in the novel with the ferocity which is used to defend property, from the moment that Catherine is savaged by Skulker, the Linton's bulldog, to the complex wresting of property by Heathcliff in the second part of the novel.

In social terms the Heights can be read as embodying the world of the gentleman farmer: the petty-bourgeois yeoman, whereas the Grange epitomises the gentry. Eagleton argues that Heathcliff's social relation to both the Heights and the Grange is one of the most complex issues in the novel. Heathcliff fiercely highlights the contradictions between the two worlds in opposing the Grange and undermining the Heights. He embodies a passionate human protest against the marriage market values of both the Heights and the Grange, while violently caricaturing precisely those values in his calculatedly callous marriage to Isabella. In this Heathcliff can be seen to be a parody of capitalist activity, yet he is not simply this, for he is also a product of and participant in that system. The contradiction of the novel is that Heathcliff both embodies and antagonises the values which he wishes to contest.

The ending of the novel with its ostensible integration of the values of the two worlds might seem to qualify Eagleton's argument that the contradictions of the novel coexist in an exciting and productive tension. However, he argues that this conclusion depends upon how one reads Hareton Earnshaw. If Hareton is read as a surrogate and diluted Heathcliff, then the novel's ending does indeed suggest a reconciliation between the gentry and the capitalist. If however, Hareton is read as a literal survivor of yeoman stock, then what effectively happens is that he is entirely conquered by the hegemony of the Grange.

Eagleton concludes that the history of Catherine and Heathcliff is the history of a social and ideological opposition between the real and the ideal which demonstrates the terror and apathy of social conditions which deny passion, and equally displays the splendour and impotence of a love which has no social basis.

FEMINIST

Feminist readings of this novel include: Joseph Boone's *Tradition, Countertradition: Love and the Form of Fiction*; Sandra Gilbert and Susan Gubar's *The Madwoman in the Attic: the Woman Writer and the Nineteenth-Century Literary Imagination*; Margaret Homan's essay 'The Name of the Mother in *Wuthering Heights*'; Carol Senf's essay 'Emily Brontë's version of **Feminist** History: *Wuthering Heights*'; and Patricia Yaeger's essay 'Violence in the Sitting Room: *Wuthering Heights* and the Woman's Novel'.

In *The Madwoman in the Attic*, Gilbert and Gubar interrogate *Wuthering Heights* in terms of what they term 'feminist mythologies'. They see the project of the novel as rewriting and revising of the Miltonic myth of the Fall. They also identify the novel as a distinctively nineteenth-century response to the problems of origins, and as an exploration into the nature of heaven and hell.

Their essay on *Wuthering Heights* sees the opposition of nature and culture in traditionally gendered terms, with culture as male, and nature as female. Indeed they assert that this novel is 'gender-obsessed'. Within the novel, a reading of the gendering of nature as female is supported by the manifestation of the storm as a female witch-child, the original Catherine, in Lockwood's second visionary dream. Heaven and hell are seen in similarly gendered terms. Catherine's choice of culture over nature, in marrying Edgar is overlaid by her assertion that she has 'no more business to marry Edgar Linton than I have to be in Heaven' (p. 80).

Their essay goes on to discuss the relationship between nature and culture in terms of Cathy and Heathcliff and their positions in the family structure. They read Heathcliff as the figurative manifestation of Catherine's desire for a whip. As Catherine's whip Heathcliff is an alternative self for her: 'a complementary addition to her being who fleshes out all her lacks' (p. 265). This is something Catherine herself recognises in her speech to Nelly Dean. Similarly Hindley's frustrated desire for a fiddle is symbolically fulfilled by his marriage to Frances.

This sustained gendered reading of the novel sees Thrushcross Grange as cultured and genteel, and the polar opposite of Wuthering Heights. That Catherine emerges from the Grange 'a lady' is seen as an inevitable consequence of subjection to masculine mythologies about heaven.

Focusing on the issue of naming in the novel, Gilbert and Gubar suggest that the writing of the name Catherine in its various manifestations, which Lockwood encounters inscribed into the windowsill, reveals the crucial lack of identity that is common to all women under patriarchy:

> What Catherine, or any girl must learn is that she does not know her own name, and therefore cannot know who she is or whom she is destined to be. (p. 276)

If Heathcliff is read as Catherine's complementary self, then, they argue Catherine's 'fall' into being a lady is accompanied by Heathcliff's diminution into a position of equally powerless femaleness. This reading of Heathcliff as female seems to go against the grain of conventional critical agreement that he epitomises heroic masculinity, especially when compared with the fair, slim, soft Edgar. But when these characters are read in terms of their social power, Heathcliff has no social position, and Edgar is always referred to as 'the master'. Edgar, who is most at home in the library, has all the power of masculine culture behind him. His mastery is contained in documents, books, rent-rolls, patriarchal domination. Edgar is the guardian of culture. Heathcliff is feminine in the sense that he is unpropertied, dispossessed, subject to the rule of the father, an outcast.

However, as Gilbert and Gubar point out, although Heathcliff can be read as Catherine's other self, he is not her identical double. This was a point first made by Leo Bersani in his book *A Future for Astyanax*. Not only is he male and she female, but he is a survivor, and usurper of power while she is a mournful, outcast, ghost. Nevertheless his fate at the end of the novel mirrors hers: he is unable to eat; he is feverish, and obsessed by the elements; and as is made clear in Gilbert and Gubar's argument, his death is partly as a result of his encounter with culture, in the form of Cathy, who embodies the intervention of patriarchy, as Edgar Linton's daughter. And in death, Heathcliff has arranged that his body shall merge with Catherine's until they are indistinguishable.

Gilbert and Gubar conclude that in writing *Wuthering Heights*, Emily Brontë struggled to subvert some of the founding myths of literature and religion, gender and marriage, patriarchy and power.

PART SEVEN

BROADER PERSPECTIVES

FURTHER READING

THE TEXT

Hilda Marsden and Ian Jack, eds., *Wuthering Heights*, Clarendon Press, 1976

Linda H. Peterson, ed., *Wuthering Heights: Case Studies in Contemporary Criticism*, Bedford Books of St. Martin's Press, 1992

William M. Sale Jr and Richard J. Dunn, eds., *Wuthering Heights*: A Norton Critical Edition, 3rd edition, W.W. Norton, 1990

BIOGRAPHY

Edward Chitham, *A Life of Emily Brontë*, Basil Blackwell, 1987

Elizabeth Gaskell, *The Life of Charlotte Brontë*, Smith, Elder & Co., London, 1857, reprinted by Penguin Books, 1975

Winifred Gérin, *Emily Brontë*, Clarendon Press, 1971

Katherine Frank, *Emily Brontë: A Chainless Soul*, H. Hamilton, 1990, paperback, Penguin Books, Harmondsworth, 1992

CRITICAL WORKS

Miriam Allott, ed., *Emily Brontë: Wuthering Heights: A Selection of Critical Essays* (Casebook Series) Macmillan, 1970

Miriam Allott, ed., *The Brontës: The Critical Heritage*, Routledge & Kegan Paul, 1974

Leo Bersani, *A Future for Astyanax: Character and Desire in Literature*, Little, 1976

Harold Bloom, ed., *Emily Brontë's Wuthering Heights*, Chelsea, 1987

Joseph Allen Boone, *Tradition, Countertradition: Love and the Form of Fiction*, University of Chicago Press, 1987

David Cecil, *Victorian Novelists: Essays in Revaluation*, revised edition, University of Chicago Press, 1958

Stevie Davies, *Emily Brontë: The Artist as a Free Woman*, Carcanet Press, 1983

Terry Eagleton, *Myths of Power: A Marxist Study of the Brontës*, Harper & Row, 1975, 2nd edition, Macmillan, 1992

Sandra Gilbert and Susan Gubar, *The Madwoman in the Attic: The Woman Writer and the Nineteenth-Century Literary Imagination*, Yale University Press, 1979

Ian Gregor, ed., *The Brontës: A Collection of Critical Essays*, Prentice-Hall, 1970

Barbara Hardy, *Forms of Feeling in Victorian Fiction*, Peter Owen, 1985

Margaret Homans, *Women Writers and Poetic Identity: Dorothy Wordsworth, Emily Brontë and Emily Dickinson*, Princeton University Press, 1980

E. Jolly, ed., *The Life and Letters of Sydney Dobell*, volume 1, Smith, 1878

Arnold Kettle, *An Introduction to the English Novel*, volume 1, Hutchinson, 1951; revised edition, Heinemann Educational and Open University Press, 1981

F.R. Leavis and Q.D. Leavis, *Lectures in America*, Pantheon Books, 1969

Margaret Lenta, 'Capitalism or Patriarchy and Immoral Love: A Study of *Wuthering Heights*', *Theoria: A Journal of Studies in the Arts, Humanities and Social Sciences*, 62, 1984, pp. 63–76

J. Hillis Miller, *Fiction and Repetition*, Harvard University Press, and Basil Blackwell, 1982

Carol A. Senf, 'Emily Brontë's version of Feminist History: *Wuthering Heights*', *Essays in Literature*, 12, 1985, pp. 201–14

Elaine Showalter, *A Literature of Their Own: British Women Novelists from*

Brontë to Lessing, Princeton University Press, 1977; revised edition, Virago, 1984

Dorothy Van Ghent, *The English Novel: Form and Function*, Harper Torchbooks, 1961

Mary Visick, *The Genesis of Wuthering Heights*, Hong Kong University Press/Oxford University Press, 1958; 3rd edition, Ian Hodgkins, 1980

Raymond Williams, *The English Novel from Dickens to Lawrence*, Chatto & Windus, 1970

David Wilson, '*Emily Brontë*: First of the Moderns,' *Modern Quarterly Miscellany*, 1, 1947, pp. 94–115

Patricia Yaeger, 'Violence in the Sitting Room: *Wuthering Heights* and the Woman's Novel', *Genre*, 21, 1988 pp. 203–29

History	Author's life	Literature
		1811 Jane Austen, *Sense and Sensibility*
		1817 Lord Byron, *Manfred*. Sir Walter Scott, *Rob Roy*
	1818 Born in Yorkshire	**1818** Mary Shelley, *Frankenstein*. Lord Byron, *Childe Harold* (Canto IV)
		1819-24 Lord Byron, *Don Juan*
	1821 Her mother dies and she is sent to Cowan Bridge School as a boarder	
1825 First passenger railway opens	**1825** Emily's two elder sisters die of consumption at Cowan Bridge School and Emily and her sister Charlotte return to Haworth where they are brought up by their aunt	
		1830 William Cobbett, *Rural Rides*
1834 Parish workhouses introduced. Abolition of slavery in territories governed by Britain		
	1835 Attends Roe Head School to study to become a teacher but is physically homesick and returns to Haworth	
1837 The Victorian era begins. Victoria becomes Queen	**1837** Spends six months as a governess at a girls' boarding school at Law Hill near Halifax, before returning home through ill health	
1838-42 Chartism is at its peak of popularity		**1838** Elizabeth Barrett Browning, *The Seraphim and Other Poems*
1842 Employment in mines of women and children under ten is outlawed. Chartist uprising	**1842** Goes to Brussels with Charlotte but aunt dies and they return home	**1842** Robert Browning, *Dramatic Lyrics*
	1846 Emily and her sisters publish a book of poems under the pseudonyms Currer, Ellis and Acton Bell	
	1847 *Wuthering Heights*	
	1848 Brother Bramwell dies; Emily dies from tuberculosis	

Byronic hero characteristically both glamourous and dangerous, haunted by the guilt of mysterious crimes

deconstruction a post-structuralist approach to literature initiated by the theoretical ideas of Jacques Derrida. Deconstruction posits the radical undecidability of all texts

discourse discourse theory is associated with the writings of Michel Foucault. Discourse generally refers to the language in which a specific area of knowledge is discussed, e.g. the discourse of law or medicine

feminist criticism there are many different forms of feminist criticism: some critics suggest ways of reading which draw attention to the patriarchal assumptions underpinning cultural production; others focus on the rediscovery of works by women writers; still others concentrate on the psychological and linguistic opportunities for women in a male-dominated culture

formalism also known as new criticism, formalists concentrate on the formal structure of the text, particularly such elements as imagery, symbolism, repetition

gothic a genre of writing which has a number of typical elements such ghosts, horror, sublime landscapes

hegemony associated with the political writings of Antonio Gramsci, hegemony refers to the web of ideologies that shape people's view of the world

ideology a set of beliefs about the world which seems both natural and inevitable.

marxist criticism a way of reading texts that focuses upon their material and historical conditions

metaphysical visionary writing, generally associated with the seventeenth century. Incorporeal, abstract

new criticism see formalism

palimpsest a text that is overwritten with other narratives and messages

parable a story which explains something which cannot easily be rendered otherwise

post-structuralism both a continuation and a critique of structuralism. Post-structuralist criticism expands the possibilities of language: the binary oppositions central to a structuralist position proliferate into innummerable alternatives . In post-structuralist readings meaning is never stable and uncontrovertible, but always provisional and contradictory

y

pseudonym an adopted name under which to write

psychoanalytic criticism a way of considering texts in terms of the psychoanalytic theories of Sigmund Freud. Emphasis upon dream analysis. Later psychoanalytic theory takes account of the work of Jacques Lacan, especially his theories of language

romantic a literary form characterised by a conscious preoccupation with the subjective and imaginative aspects of life

semiotics the study of signs and sign systems. Associated particularly with the work of Ferdinand de Saussure

structuralism structuralist criticism derives from the linguistic theory of Saussure. It focuses on the internal structures of language which permit a text to 'mean' something. A structuralist analysis posits language rather than an individual author as the creator of meaning – no word has intrinsic meaning, in and of itself – it only means something in relation to other words. This insight is discussed chiefly in terms of binary oppositions. We understand what 'hot' means only in relation to the term 'cold'. According to structuralists writing has no origin – every individual utterance is already preceded by language

transcendent often synonymous with metaphysical – that which is beyond the limits of human cognition; exceeding or surpassing the ordinary

AUTHOR OF THIS NOTE

Claire Jones attended the universities of Sussex and Oxford. She has taught in Cape Town and Oxford, and is now a lecturer in English literary studies at the University of Luton, where she specialises in literary theory and contemporary literature. She has published one work of fiction and is currently writing a book on postcolonial literary theory.

Notes

Notes

Notes

Notes

Notes

York Notes Advanced (£3.99 each)

Margaret Atwood
The Handmaid's Tale

Jane Austen
Emma

Jane Austen
Pride and Prejudice

William Blake
Songs of Innocence and of Experience

Charlotte Brontë
Jane Eyre

Emily Brontë
Wuthering Heights

Geoffrey Chaucer
The Wife of Bath's Prologue and Tale

Joseph Conrad
Heart of Darkness

Charles Dickens
Great Expectations

F. Scott Fitzgerald
The Great Gatsby

Thomas Hardy
Tess of the d'Urbervilles

Seamus Heaney
Selected Poems

James Joyce
Dubliners

Arthur Miller
Death of a Salesman

William Shakespeare
Antony and Cleopatra

William Shakespeare
Hamlet

William Shakespeare
King Lear

William Shakespeare
The Merchant of Venice

William Shakespeare
Much Ado About Nothing

William Shakespeare
Othello

William Shakespeare
Romeo and Juliet

William Shakespeare
The Tempest

Mary Shelley
Frankenstein

Alice Walker
The Color Purple

Tennessee Williams
A Streetcar Named Desire

John Webster
The Duchess of Malfi

GCSE and equivalent levels (£3.50 each)

Harold Brighouse
Hobson's Choice

Charles Dickens
Great Expectations

Charles Dickens
Hard Times

George Eliot
Silas Marner

William Golding
Lord of the Flies

Thomas Hardy
The Mayor of Casterbridge

Susan Hill
I'm the King of the Castle

Barry Hines
A Kestrel for a Knave

Harper Lee
To Kill a Mockingbird

Arthur Miller
A View from the Bridge

Arthur Miller
The Crucible

George Orwell
Animal Farm

J.B. Priestley
An Inspector Calls

J.D. Salinger
The Catcher in the Rye

William Shakespeare
Macbeth

William Shakespeare
The Merchant of Venice

William Shakespeare
Romeo and Juliet

William Shakespeare
Twelfth Night

George Bernard Shaw
Pygmalion

John Steinbeck
Of Mice and Men

Mildred D. Taylor
Roll of Thunder, Hear My Cry

James Watson
Talking in Whispers

A Choice of Poets

Nineteenth Century Short Stories

Poetry of the First World War

Chinua Achebe
Things Fall Apart

Edward Albee
Who's Afraid of Virginia Woolf?

Maya Angelou
I Know Why The Caged Bird Sings

Jane Austen
Mansfield Park

Jane Austen
Northanger Abbey

Jane Austen
Persuasion

Jane Austen
Pride and Prejudice

Jane Austen
Sense and Sensibility

Samuel Beckett
Waiting for Godot

John Betjeman
Selected Poems

Robert Bolt
A Man for All Seasons

Charlotte Brontë
Jane Eyre

Emily Brontë
Wuthering Heights

Robert Burns
Selected Poems

Lord Byron
Selected Poems

Geoffrey Chaucer
The Franklin's Tale

Geoffrey Chaucer
The Knight's Tale

Geoffrey Chaucer
The Merchant's Tale

Geoffrey Chaucer
The Miller's Tale

Geoffrey Chaucer
The Nun's Priest's Tale

Geoffrey Chaucer
The Pardoner's Tale

Geoffrey Chaucer
Prologue to the Canterbury Tales

Samuel Taylor Coleridge
Selected Poems

Daniel Defoe
Moll Flanders

Daniel Defoe
Robinson Crusoe

Shelagh Delaney
A Taste of Honey

Charles Dickens
Bleak House

Charles Dickens
David Copperfield

Charles Dickens
Oliver Twist

Emily Dickinson
Selected Poems

John Donne
Selected Poems

Douglas Dunn
Selected Poems

George Eliot
Middlemarch

George Eliot
The Mill on the Floss

T.S. Eliot
The Waste Land

T.S. Eliot
Selected Poems

Henry Fielding
Joseph Andrews

E.M. Forster
Howards End

E.M. Forster
A Passage to India

John Fowles
The French Lieutenant's Woman

Elizabeth Gaskell
North and South

Oliver Goldsmith
She Stoops to Conquer

Graham Greene
Brighton Rock

Graham Greene
The Heart of the Matter

Graham Greene
The Power and the Glory

Willis Hall
The Long and the Short and the Tall

Thomas Hardy
Far from the Madding Crowd

Thomas Hardy
Jude the Obscure

Thomas Hardy
The Return of the Native

Thomas Hardy
Selected Poems

Thomas Hardy
Tess of the d'Urbervilles

L.P. Hartley
The Go-Between

Nathaniel Hawthorne
The Scarlet Letter

Seamus Heaney
Selected Poems

Ernest Hemingway
A Farewell to Arms

Ernest Hemingway
The Old Man and the Sea

Homer
The Iliad

Homer
The Odyssey

Gerard Manley Hopkins
Selected Poems

Ted Hughes
Selected Poems

Aldous Huxley
Brave New World

Henry James
Portrait of a Lady

Ben Jonson
The Alchemist

Ben Jonson
Volpone

James Joyce
A Portrait of the Artist as a Young Man

John Keats
Selected Poems

Philip Larkin
Selected Poems

D.H. Lawrence
The Rainbow

D.H. Lawrence
Selected Stories

D.H. Lawrence
Sons and Lovers

D.H. Lawrence
Women in Love

Louise Lawrence
Children of the Dust

Laurie Lee
Cider with Rosie

Christopher Marlowe
Doctor Faustus

John Milton
Paradise Lost Bks I & II

John Milton
Paradise Lost IV & IX

Robert O'Brien
Z for Zachariah

Sean O'Casey
Juno and the Paycock

George Orwell
Nineteen Eighty-four

John Osborne
Look Back in Anger

Wilfred Owen
Selected Poems

Harold Pinter
The Caretaker

Sylvia Plath
Selected Works

Alexander Pope
Selected Poems

Jean Rhys
Wide Sargasso Sea

Willy Russell
Educating Rita

Willy Russell
Our Day Out

William Shakespeare
As You Like It

William Shakespeare
Coriolanus

William Shakespeare
Henry IV Pt 1

William Shakespeare
Henry IV Pt II

William Shakespeare
Henry V

William Shakespeare
Julius Caesar

William Shakespeare
Measure for Measure

William Shakespeare
A Midsummer Night's Dream

William Shakespeare
Richard II

William Shakespeare
Richard III

William Shakespeare
Sonnets

William Shakespeare
The Taming of the Shrew

William Shakespeare
The Tempest

William Shakespeare
The Winter's Tale

George Bernard Shaw
Arms and the Man

George Bernard Shaw
Saint Joan

Richard Brinsley Sheridan
The Rivals

R.C. Sherriff
Journey's End

Rukshana Smith
Salt on the Snow

Muriel Spark
The Prime of Miss Jean Brodie

John Steinbeck
The Grapes of Wrath

John Steinbeck
The Pearl

R.L. Stevenson
Dr Jekyll and Mr Hyde

Tom Stoppard
Rosencrantz and Guildenstern are Dead

Jonathan Swift
Gulliver's Travels

Robert Swindells
Daz 4 Zoe

John Millington Synge
The Playboy of the Western World

W.M. Thackeray
Vanity Fair

Mark Twain
Huckleberry Finn

Virgil
The Aeneid

Derek Walcott
Selected Poems

Oscar Wilde
The Importance of Being Earnest

Tennessee Williams
Cat on a Hot Tin Roof

Tennessee Williams
The Glass Menagerie

Virginia Woolf
Mrs Dalloway

Virginia Woolf
To the Lighthouse

William Wordsworth
Selected Poems

W.B. Yeats
Selected Poems

Six Women Poets

York Notes – the Ultimate Literature Guides

York Notes are recognised as the best literature study guides.
If you have enjoyed using this book and have found it useful, you
can now order others directly from us – simply follow the ordering
instructions below.

HOW TO ORDER

Decide which title(s) you require and then order in one of the following
ways:

Booksellers
All titles available from good bookstores.

By post
List the title(s) you require in the space provided overleaf,
select your method of payment, complete your name and
address details and return your completed order form and
payment to:

> *Addison Wesley Longman Ltd*
> *PO BOX 88*
> *Harlow*
> *Essex CM19 5SR*

By phone
Call our Customer Information Centre on 01279 623923 to
place your order, quoting mail number: HEYN1.

By fax
Complete the order form overleaf, ensuring you fill in your
name and address details and method of payment, and fax it
to us on 01279 414130.

By e-mail
E-mail your order to us on awlhe.orders@awl.co.uk listing
title(s) and quantity required and providing full name and
address details as requested overleaf. Please quote mail
number: HEYN1. Please do not send credit card details by
e-mail.

York Notes Order Form

Titles required:

Quantity	Title/ISBN	Price

Sub total _____

Please add £2.50 postage & packing _____

(P & P is free for orders over £50) _____

Total _____

Mail no: HEYN1

Your Name _____

Your Address _____

_____

Postcode _____ Telephone _____

Method of payment

☐ I enclose a cheque or a P/O for £_____ made payable to Addison Wesley Longman Ltd

☐ Please charge my Visa/Access/AMEX/Diners Club card
Number _____ Expiry Date _____
Signature _____ Date _____

(please ensure that the address given above is the same as for your credit card)

Prices and other details are correct at time of going to press but may change without notice. All orders are subject to status.

☐ *Please tick this box if you would like a complete listing of Longman Study Guides (suitable for GCSE and A-level students)*

🌑 York Press

▦ Longman

Addison
Wesley
Longman